1979

ON THE FOUR QUARTETS OF T S ELIOT

ON THE FOUR QUARTETS
OF T S ELIOT

CONSTANCE DE MASIREVICH

WITH A FOREWORD BY
ROY CAMPBELL

LONDON
VINCENT STUART
MCMLXV

FIRST PUBLISHED IN 1953
SECOND IMPRESSION 1965
BY VINCENT STUART PUBLISHERS LTD
45 LOWER BELGRAVE STREET LONDON SW1

PUBLISHED IN THE UNITED STATES
BY BARNES & NOBLE, INC.
NEW YORK

Reproduced and printed in Great Britain by
Latimer Trend & Co. Ltd., Whitstable

To You
Lady of the Promontory of Pitecusa
Protect the vagrant seafarer
Fold the returning in Your golden robe.

FOREWORD

LITERARY CRITICISM in England has been slowly changing its function from the expression of free individual views in the assessment, appreciation, and encouragement of talent, to the expression of a collective, official view which is more concerned with the regulation, standardisation, administration, and rationing of talent (and even of experience). A special sort of officialese jargon has been evolved which is as far from the vernacular, and as difficult for the ordinary educated man to understand, as the jargon used on ministry forms: and quite as meaningless. The current phrases of this officialese jargon – 'new awareness', 'new synthesis', 'overtones', 'undertones', etc. – lose any meaning they ever had after the third or fourth time they are used, but they remain in currency, like those ancient Inca words that were shrieked to the explorer Fernandez by the hypercentenarian cockatoo in the Andes some century or so after the language and those who spoke it had become extinct. They remain in circulation, since their automatic use by literary officials gives the latter the hallucination that they are employed *for some purpose other* than that of merely being employed. Were it not that they were supplied with catch-phrases that they can learn parrot-wise, they would not be able to utter any phrases at all. And that is why the body of critical literature today is so vast in bulk compared with that of any other period in literature, and yet so puny in content.

Before the present state of critical *rigor mortis* set in, Eliot had already become accepted as the norm of English poetry. What was extraordinary about it was that he *was* actually the best poet writing in England at the time when he imposed his pattern on English poetical thought. That was chiefly a matter of luck for us as well as for himself. At similar periods of literary decline, it has often been the worst, or one of the worst, poets who sets his impress on the period: and this period, being what it was, did not

7

deserve such miraculous luck by any means. But for a few exceptions, Eliot's pre-eminence was to be measured by the bulk rather than the variety or perceptiveness of the adulatory critical literature which surrounded him. He was praised for the very opposite qualities to those for which his work was so remarkable. As the accepted norm, he came to be identified forcibly with all those things for which the uncreative majority stood – mere innovation for its own sake, scepticism, boredom, listlessness, and revolt. In almost everything written about Eliot for many years, after having read the first paragraph one can more or less reproduce the rest of the page verbatim, so stereotyped has this type of literature become in thought and phraseology. It is very rarely that one comes across the direct personal approach to poetry, without any stereotyped collective formulas.

This book is an example of the independent personal approach. It is full of deep thought, conviction, and what is even rarer in a modern critical work, real human charm. The author, in spiritual and intellectual outlook, is far out of the rut in which collective criticism has stuck. The warmth and enthusiasm with which this essay is written is generated and controlled by a very clear judgment indeed.

Such lively and fresh personal reactions to Mr. Eliot's poetry stimulate and renew one's own. After reading this essay I went back to the *Four Quartets* with fresh curiosity and derived fresh pleasure and strength from them: and I feel sure that most other lovers and admirers of the work of our finest living poet will derive similar pleasure from seeing it through the eyes of such a clear-headed enthusiast as the writer of this book.

Roy Campbell

INTRODUCTION

THE PRESENT ESSAY is meant as an interpretation; it is not a literary critical essay, but a guide to the inner meaning of an incomparable poem and it is intended to encourage readers of T. S. Eliot to undertake the exploration for themselves. The literary criticism of the present subject lies outside my competence, and has been admirably dealt with by Miss Helen Gardner in her book *The Art of T. S. Eliot*, to which I owe much information and many useful indications. I am aware that the meaning as I see it will be an aspect, or part of a meaning which I feel to be inexhaustible. I am conscious of having given no more than 'hints and guesses' in the hope that they, on the reader's part, will be followed by the hints and guesses of his own discoveries. I had read the poem often but found, in the process of writing, many new visions, and special surprises in the discovery of how the structure of thought is fitted at the joints, each movement following and completing that which preceded it. I believe this work to be something which has been missing in Western literature since the inauguration of the age of reason, a manual of the spiritual life which is, at the same time, an integral part of the great literature of a people. Whether a man be an agnostic, or member of any of the existing churches will not matter. Though the poet uses Christian symbols and takes much from classical sources this is chiefly a poem about psychology, and besides the known symbols of our tradition it introduces speculations from the field of modern mathematics. The reader will be justified in wanting to know what my qualifications are for undertaking so exalted a task. I have no scholarly qualifications. I have had experiences of the kind the poem deals with, and am trying to live by the light they shed on life. I am not a professional writer. The motive for writing this essay has been that, to my knowledge, nobody else has written it, and because I feel that it might prove helpful to some reader.

The starting point of the *Four Quartets* is a moment of illumination during which some insight into the nature of time has been gained. The subject of the *Four Quartets* is consciousness, more especially time as a form of consciousness, or the human consciousness in time, and the path of liberation from time by growing into new dimensions. The poem is divided into four parts, or Quartets, each in turn being written in movements of varying lengths and rhythms. Each Quartet is written under the sign of one of the four elements. Fluid, dark, blazing, translucent, in perpetual change the four elements, new as on the morning of creation, spin from the poet's loom; threading the fabric of the poem, suggesting the world as it presents itself to sensual perception, the edifice of our three-dimensional vision in time. Having 'purified the dialect of the tribe' and transmuted old words and phrases into new, he gives us new eyes with which to look upon this world, the length and breadth, and depth and time. Aroused from quotidian torpor through art we are prepared to receive ideas that might not otherwise have found access to our interest. The elements symbolise inner states; with the help of natural imagery mutations of the psyche are described. Each Quartet revives the same experience in a new way, and corresponds to one trial of the soul: trial through air, through earth, through water, and through fire. In each Quartet one element corresponds to one season in the phenomenal world, and to one phase in the noumenal world of man's inner growth.

Burnt Norton, the first Quartet, derives its name from an anonymous English cottage and garden. It is a poem about incidental illumination. Description having been replaced by gradually introduced suggestion of the scene, an atmosphere of secretiveness and enchantment is created. The house is closed, the formal garden empty: a still place on a still warm day. The garden is hedged in, we are unaware of the surroundings, the sea is far away.

The second Quartet, *East Coker*, is called after a village in Somersetshire from which in the seventeenth century,

T. S. Eliot's ancestor set out for the New World. Through images of rural life enchantment is replaced by down-to-earth earthness, and we are made aware of nature, the bondage of time, and recurrence within the circle of time. The village opens out on the fields and the sea-breeze is in the air. Initial illumination was given freely but what may follow is 'hard and bitter death'. The poet ponders on liberation from time and realises the difficulty of the way. A feeling of the coming journey is introduced.

The *Dry Salvages*, the third Quartet, tells about the journey. It is a poem of adventure. The name is derived from a group of rocky islands off the coast of New England where T. S. Eliot lived as a child. The voyage of man is his life; it is a perilous journey along time, amidst infinity, in search of rebirth through sacrifice. But the traveller does not know his goal. Both perpetual journeying or shipwreck are possibilities, but there are intimations of a home-coming.

With the fourth and concluding Quartet, *Little Gidding*, we return to England once more. Little Gidding, a small Huntingdonshire village was the scene of happenings that had in them the elements of both history and legend. For twenty years Nicholas Ferrar lived there with his family and friends, and the fame of their good life spread far and wide. What were the ideals and rules by which these people lived? They were Christians, but why did this man leave such a deep imprint on his place and time, and that at a period when the devout life was far from being as uncommon as it is today, and when religious orders and churchmen's influence were live factors in cultural life? The last Quartet is a poem of home-coming. The poet visits the chapel on a winter afternoon. A way has been found, and it leads back to our beginning. Again, as in the first Quartet, but intensified, and one might say, solidified, the element of illumination prevails.

Since the *Four Quartets* constitute a poem about time it may be useful here to survey the findings of modern mathematics as taught at universities today, in so far as they affect the present subject. It has become an established axiom that time is the fourth dimension. At this axiom we arrive by the following process of reasoning:

A point has no dimensions.

The first dimension is the movement of a point in space, a line.

The second dimension is the movement of a line in space, a surface.

The third dimension is the movement of a surface in space, a three-dimensional body possessing length, breadth and depth.

The fourth dimension is the movement of a three-dimensional body in space, a four-dimensional body, or a three-dimensional body's time.

For each additional dimension the preceding dimension will be a falsification of reality, true on its own plane, false for the subsequent.

To put it differently:

A line is the movement of a point in space, a figure of one-dimension.

A surface is the movement of a line in space, a figure of two dimensions.

A three-dimensional body is the movement of a surface in space, a figure of three dimensions.

A four-dimensional body is the movement of a three-dimensional body in space, its time, or better still, duration.

Intense pre-occupation with the problem of time as a form of consciousness, and with occurring different apprehensions of time is the starting point of the *Four Quartets*. Man, in relation to the third and fourth dimensions, is indeed a strange border-case. In his ordinary state he hovers around the cross-section of time, the now. T. S. Eliot calls it the intersection of time. If time exists spatially, and if, moreover, we abandon determinism and admit possible variations in coming events, we are wanderers in a higher dimensional universe, but our perception shows us a fraction of the journey, the now, or the before, but not normally a vision of simultaneity. Childhood, maturity, old age, a man would have to experience in simultaneity; that would be four-dimensional vision. Imagine the life of the universe in such vision. It would be impossible, three-dimensional consciousness would burst under the pressure. The present and the past of a man's life, and various episodes within that past do not co-exist in consciousness; while the ray plays on one instant, the others are in the dark. Simultaneity is a property of the higher dimension. We must remember that in many philosophies individuation, the source of separatism and thus desire, or call it incarnation, is considered as an illusion of the mind, the original fall, or nescience of the east. There is, in the manifestations of man's higher activities, ample evidence that, under certain conditions, the mind may transcend the limitations of time and enter a new mode of being. The artist in Eliot has discovered that the entrance into a new world, which is 'the old world made explicit, understood', lies on the cross-section of the now. Only the now, the present moment consciously lived, can become an entrance into a condition beyond time, where the world is experienced on a new plane. Later in the poem the condition of simultaneity felt during a state of high tension and fuller awareness is analysed. The taste of ecstasy accompanies a widening of the field of vision. But in itself the spatial pattern of all existing joys and agonies is no solution. The goal moves further off. From each subsequent plane, being moves on to a fuller understanding by giving up a former truth. The key to the thought of T. S. Eliot is the idea of sacrifice as a means of becoming, of birth through death, and on this theme he gives us countless variations.

In conversation and writings one sometimes comes across the opinion that T. S. Eliot is a sad, negative person. It always seems to me that the almost deliberate ignoring of the great positive aspects of his poetry comes from something small and afraid in man, something which desires no change, something which wishes everything to remain as it is.

BURNT NORTON

THE POEM starts from a definite point in space and a definite moment in time. *Burnt Norton*, the cottage not now inhabited, the formal garden still under the heat, peopled by memories only of 'what has been, and what might have been', suggests the mind of the poet in reverie that leads to his thinking about time in a crescendo of concentration. Perhaps this is a place where he might have found human happiness, and his mind dwelling on what might have been, conceived the beautiful image of the children hidden in the foliage, eager with suppressed laughter. Stillness, solitude, beauty both natural and civilised; the three are conducive to illumination.

The first movement begins with reflection on the nature of time in this enchanted place. A strange idea is introduced. Not only are past and future co-existent with the present; equally existent in some unknown mode are the non-actualised possibilities of each moment. These possibilities the poet has introduced into his scheme of time.

> 'Time present and time past
> Are both perhaps present in time future,
> And time future contained in time past'.

The idea of co-existent time as a pattern in higher space implies that our consciousness moves through this pattern as a traveller, arriving and departing with each moment. The yesterday exists, as the city we left yesterday does exist. The morrow exists, as several possible goals exist for our tomorrow. Nothing is excluded. All is. The actualised and the non-actualised both exist.

> 'Footfalls echo in the memory
> Down the passage which we did not take
> Towards the door we never opened
> Into the rose-garden. My words echo
> Thus, in your mind.
>   But to what purpose

Disturbing the dust on a bowl of rose-leaves
I do not know'.

The value of this idea is difficult to assess. One can only say that it enriches the picture of the world in some undefinable way, being like a glimpse of something multi-dimensional and complete. It is like a fleeting impression of some multi-foliate flower, a pattern both still and in motion, exfoliate, returning within itself.

The images that evoke the setting are chosen to suggest the phases of a psychic process. 'Dust on dead rose-leaves', 'dry pool, dry concrete', 'drained pool', and the 'empty alleys' signify the ordinary state, in which the 'now' is not fully realised, which is aridity, dream, and death. Then the bird calls:

'Quick, said the bird, find them, find them',

answering the 'hidden laughter of the children': We are now on the verge of another state.

'Dry the pool, dry concrete, brown edged,
And the pool was filled with water out of sunlight,
And the lotus rose, quietly, quietly,
The surface glittered out of heart of light'.

It is the pinpoint of illumination expanding into the incommunicable. The moment passes, the vision recedes.

'Then a cloud passed, and the pool was empty.
Go, said the bird, for the leaves were full of children,
Hidden excitedly, containing laughter.
Go, go, go, said the bird: human kind
Cannot bear very much reality.
Time past and time future
What might have been and what has been
Point to one end, which is always present'.

The laughter of the children hidden in the trees; something which exists, joy and innocence, so near that we can almost touch it, yet hidden from our sight; near and elusive in human happiness which resembles the special state as reflection does true form, nearer and still elusive in the special state itself. But after the call there sounds a note of warning; it is something too potent to be borne by man, in his ordinary condition.

Already here the nucleus of the poet's philosophy declares itself. Intuition about the real nature of time came in one instant, a 'now' of intense life in concentration. The concentration is upon time not as something abstract, outside ourselves, but as our own most intimate being. Everything is in the mind: time and beyond time, hell and heaven, death and life. The key to understanding is awareness in the now. The poet will return to the theme in a moment, and will not abandon it to the end. But awareness of the moment in the moment is not a state that comes naturally to man. Usually, if at all, it comes and goes, elusively, with happiness or suffering, it comes with the creative urge, in abstract thought, through the love of God, or the love of creations. Movement two will be an approach to a description of the special state. Movement three returns to man's ordinary condition, and to a possible remedy of this mortal illness of our perceptions.

In the second movement the poet's positive attitude is like a soaring gesture. The juxtaposition of contraries, which runs through the whole mature work of T. S. Eliot, is taken up with great force and precision at the opening, and right through the second part of the second movement.

'Garlic and sapphires in the mud
Clot the bedded axle-tree'.

We live with the intolerable conflict of our dualistic nature, victims to inertia, weighed down by struggles that rend us, but ever and anon the force that moves the sun and all the stars will reassert itself.

'The dance along the artery
The circulation of the lymph
Are figured in the drift of stars
Ascend to summer in the tree
We move above the moving tree

In light upon the figured leaf'.

Is this a negation of life? I think not. And the positive attitude towards the joy and the horror, the good and the bad in ourselves and in others will gradually lift us to another point of view where opposites converge, and their meaning changes in a sort of cancellation. But the reconciliation eludes logical definition.

'And hear upon the sodden floor
Below, the boarhound and the boar
Pursue their pattern as before
But reconciled among the stars'.

The drawing upward is a drawing inward. The centre of the wheel, the balance of all movement is a still place. There a discovery is made. Not the movement is the life, but the stillness. But we are talking in terms of opposites, we cannot do otherwise. There dualistic logic based on the opposition of contraries, devised at and valid at the periphery is so no longer. The stillness is the dance; is both, and is neither. Mystical writings abound with paradoxes. It is inevitable, they are concerned with translating a more inclusive, higher dimensional comprehension into the language of the more limited dimension. This is a truism, and the task seems hopeless every time. The startling effect of what, to us, seems non-sense, and, in good writing, the aesthetic shock experienced has probably acted on many individual minds, precipitating them into what can become true only through immediate experience. Few men have the experience but all men, except the perverted and diseased, have a more or less dim intuition of their latent powers. Apart from his message, purely as an artist, Eliot has a unique place in our literary world, and, it is hoped, far beyond it, in the cultural life of the world. But if his message had been completely unintelligible to men, that fame could not have increased and our understanding of him could not hope to deepen. His great poetical gift, his sympathy, humility, and good sense have shielded T. S. Eliot from the public scorn reserved for less talented mystics. And he knows that the gift is an obligation, demanding the whole of man. In the coming movement, as through the whole work, we feel his being turned towards us in an intense effort to be clear and simple enough for our understanding, and the balance struck between the demands of his art and of his philosophy is admirable.

> 'At the still point of the turning world. Neither
>   flesh nor fleshless;
> Neither from nor towards; at the still point,
>   there the dance is,
> But neither arrest nor movement. And do not call
>   it fixity,
> Where past and future are gathered. Neither
>   movement from nor towards,
> Neither ascent nor decline. Except for the point,
>   the still point,
> There would be no dance, and there is only
>   the dance'.

The following lines make it clear that time-space were momentarily left behind, if one can say that the point leaves itself behind when it turns into a line. It would be more correct to say that the point realises itself in a new manner. The approach to the enigmas of existence via mathematics may indeed eliminate the need for outside agents. Everything is within each. In this discovery the truth of religion can be re-discovered by a godless society, and its falsities, by which I mean literal and limited grasp, can be eliminated.

> 'I can only say, *there* we have been: but I cannot
>   say where.
> And I cannot say, how long, for that is to place
>   it in time.
> The inner freedom from the practical desire,
> The release from action and suffering, release
>   from the inner

And the outer compulsion, yet surrounded
By a grace of sense, a white light still and moving,
Erhebung without motion, concentration
Without elimination, both a new world
And the old made explicit, understood
In the completion of its partial ecstasy,
The resolution of its partial horror'.

The world is one indeed, only the form of perception
changes.* But our present state, the poet repeats, allows
no more than a rare illumination, if that. He then makes
an important statement which we shall have to recall to
mind later as we move on with him into meditations on
art and history.

'To be conscious is not to be in time'.

In other words, the moment of full awareness, so rare in
our lives, during which the contemplated idea, being, or
object and the contemplating mind constitute a unity,
already pertains to a new dimension. Man, at that moment
lives on the intersection of time, not in the before, or the
after as he usually does.

Whether they know it or not, it is the fullness of being
that men seek in all their pursuits. Many of these lead
further and further away from it. The sum of unaware
moments adds up to nothing; life in a fictitious world of
distractions is a meaningless nightmare. Nothing is gained
by flight into this or that, the past or the future, either our
own or that of others. Theories and utopias are ultimately
useless. To take the present by the horns and make it yield
to us, that is an overcoming of the self and will be 'fruitful
in the lives of others'.

'But only in time can the moment in the
      rose-garden,
The moment in the arbour where the rain beat,
The moment in the draughty church at smokefall

*See TERTIUM ORGANUM by P. D. Ouspensky

19

Be remembered; involved with past and future.
Only through time time is conquered'.

The third movement proceeds to examine the psychological climate in which we ordinarily live. It is a negative condition under which nothing can be done. With horror we behold the gloomy hills, dantesque and universal, a grey commonplace hell, everlastingly recurrent while man wills it.

'Neither plenitude nor vacancy. Only a flicker
Over the strained time-ridden faces
Distracted from distraction by distraction
Filled with fancies and empty of meaning,
Tumid apathy with no concentration
Men and bits of paper, whirled by the cold wind
That blows before and after time,
Wind in and out of unwholesome lungs
Time before and time after.
Eructation of unhealthy souls
Into the faded air, the torpid
Driven on the wind that sweeps the gloomy
        hills of London,
Hampstead and Clerkenwell, Campden and Putney,
Highgate, Primrose and Ludgate. Not here
Not here the darkness, in this twittering world'.

This is the vision of *The Waste Land*, where the damned souls stream over London Bridge on their way to the office and the poet exclaims, dismayed:

'I did not know death had undone so many!'

Cave and labyrinth of classical and Christian mythology did not illustrate meaningless living like the scene of this modern metropolis in the horrible sameness of all its suburbs. But then we have indeed become masters of the meaningless life, and the scenery, outward manifestation of inward conceptions, has been imagined and set up by ourselves. The next stanza brings the first mention of a way out and definite conditions. So far we have heard of accidental escape from time, or grace, and it has set off our ordinary state, which until then we thought to be perfectly normal. But conscious effort implies the idea of systematic retreat from the old and advance into something new. The negative way is a positive way. Having acknowledged our position, we are led to desire penance and mortification.

> 'Descend lower, descend only
> Into the world of perpetual solitude,
> World not world, but that which is not world,
> Internal darkness, deprivation
> And destitution of all property,
> Desiccation of the world of sense,
> Evacuation of the world of fancy,
> Inoperancy of the world of spirit;'

The philosophy of T. S. Eliot is the profound and tragical philosophy of the great religions, and of the ancient mysteries in a pagan world. The Appollonine way of day does not lead out of this dimension. The Dionysian element of crisis and dying is indispensable in order to leave the rigid mechanical rails of time, the 'metalled ways'. But we should be quite mistaken in imagining a violent and precipitated process. The useful sacrifice is that which has become inevitable. We might imagine a seed sprouting in the dark, or a dough worked by patient hands until it comes clear off the rolling board. That would be a perfect illustration of the path of liberation from time.

The fourth movement is very short and poses the question, but does not answer it, of our immortality. If we follow the way, what shall we get? Every disciple asks the question, again and again. Shall we be dust, held in the grip of gnarled roots, or shall 'the sunflower turn to us?' The question shall not be answered, nor can it be, for it is wrongly put. The perception of ourselves as separate beings is itself a negation of that other life. The Buddha's silence concerning Nirvana gave rise to crude forms of nihilism.

Christian teachings have many degenerate variations of primitive superstition, and have alienated many a good but not profound brain from religion. It cannot be otherwise. But all this is dispute by means of the logic of three dimensions.

'After the kingfisher's wing
Has answered light to light, and is silent, the
    light is still
At the still point of the turning world'.

Something given, something received. The most intimate contact in the world! The questioning is stilled forever.

The fifth movement presents the first application of the theory of higher dimensions to the phenomenon of art, and in the second half of the movement, the close of the first Quartet, to love. The subject of art has perhaps presented itself to the poet's mind as a result of the great difficulty of movement two; that of giving form to experience essentially inexpressible in our language. The theme of love comes as a natural sequel. Art demands the whole of man, and man responds by giving in love and wonder. The love is for the unknown in himself, and through it the gift reaches mankind.

The movement begins:

'Words move, music moves
Only in time; but that which is only living
Can only die. Words, after speech, reach
Into the silence. Only by the form, the pattern,
Can words or music reach
The stillness, as a Chinese jar still
Moves perpetually in its stillness.
Not the stillness of the violin, while the note lasts,
Not that only, but the co-existence,
Or say that the end precedes the beginning,
And the end and the beginning were always there
Before the beginning and after the end.
And all is always now'.

It might prove helpful at this point to introduce a mathematical design. We have spoken of figures of different dimensions. For the sake of simplicity we have probably imagined straight lines, planes, and cubes as figures of one, two, and three dimensions. In fact the line, the movement of a point in space, need not stay on a surface, but can move in any dimension. The movement of a line, and of resulting surfaces, can thus trace varying shapes in higher dimensions. Let us, for instance, take a figure of three dimensions with movement in it, say an hour-glass, and imagine it vertically traversing a figure of two dimensions, a surface. On the surface the passage of the hour-glass will be experienced as a periodically expanding and contracting disc, which will not be known to be the cross-section of an hour-glass, but will be felt to exist independently. On the other hand, for the self-feeling of the hour-glass the cross-section will hardly exist.

A work of art, for Eliot, is such a self-existing entity in higher space. It is a simultaneous pattern. Platonists and others might dispute whether the pattern exists in higher space, independently of manifestation in our space. Dimensions render this argument obsolete. Pattern and cross-section are indivisible; the pattern the tracing of the lesser dimension in a higher space; the lesser dimension nevertheless devoid of substance and reality as compared to the higher. In relation to art: the word, the single note exists only in relation to the whole, in itself we might say it has never existed. Only the pattern exists, the whole work of art, but without the parts it would be non-existent. But a sum of words, or a sum of notes of music does not constitute a work of art, though they may trace patterns unconnected with a higher life and meaningless. The work of art, as it were, has a soul which makes of a meaningless pattern significant form. Significant of what? Significant of itself always. The best paintings of birds, for instance, are probably the early Chinese and Japanese because they express the inner being of a bird; all that a bird is and could be, all that it feels, the sum of the experience of a species is compressed into a symbol with perfect economy of means. All great works of art have this sense of urgency about them and combine it with mastery of the medium of expression. The greater a master, the more acutely aware is he on the cross-section of the now, and his awareness is of the whole within the part, the higher dimension, or dimensions within the lesser. The inky smudge of a lonely crow seen through the mountain fog becomes a key to the whole universe. The contact with such works of art is like the contact with a different time, swift as the ray of light. When, at the cross-section of time, in creation or in contemplation of art, we become aware of the significance of form, we are invaded by this simultaneous time, soothed by the stillness in the movement. In conjunction with the whole the part has come to life, and now, miraculously, it does contain the whole. The detail and the present has the power to absolve us with the enchantment of a rounded harmony. The artist had the experience and gave it form, but the form ever a mere shadow of the substance. He communicates a meaning, and we in turn make it our own. Art, like love, unites men.

The poet goes on to speak now of his own work, and of the hard labour of creation.

'Words strain,
Crack and sometimes break, under the burden,
Under the tension, slip, slide, perish.
Decay with imprecision, will not stay in place,
Will not stay still'.

These are the hardships of the craft. In addition, out of ordinary consciousness come the thousand and one voices to distract the artist from his purpose. The Logos dwells in him, assaulted from within his own psyche by the confused noises of his temporal consciousnesses, those of his cells and organs, of their subjective fancies and notions; from without by the voices of others, men with world-values only, equally subjective and phantasmal. They are the men who invent meaningless patterns, who would

distract the artist from his purpose by filling the grey void
of time with their discordant noises.

> 'Shrieking voices
> Scolding, mocking, or merely chattering,
> Always assail them. The Word in the desert
> Is most attacked by voices of temptation,
> The crying shadow of the funeral dance,
> The loud lament of the disconsolate chimera'.

The first Quartet closes on a movement of love. There
is almost no transition, the metre changes to one simpler,
light and gay. The theme of higher dimensional being
lived as motion in time is continued, and is now applied
to love.

> 'The detail of the pattern is movement,
> As in the figure of ten stairs.
> Desire itself is movement
> Not in itself desirable;
> Love is itself unmoving,
> Only the cause and end of movement,
> Timeless, and undesiring
> Except in the aspect of time'.

Then a simultaneous image; the moving pattern, the
joyful reality thereof. The pattern of the world stands
revealed within the sudden ray of illumination. There is
light and joy.

> 'Sudden in a shaft of sunlight
> Even while the dust moves
> There rises the hidden laughter
> Of children in the foliage'.

Like a beseeching exhortation, the closing lines:

> 'Quick now, here, now, always –
> Ridiculous the waste sad time
> Stretching before and after'.

EAST COKER

I F THE INITIAL ILLUMINATION is given through grace, rising, as it were, from depths within man that he has never sounded and flooding his ordinary consciousness with new tremors and new visions, nevertheless everything remains to be done, and the whole way lies before man. And as in nature season follows season in unalterable rhythm, so is the path of perfection subject to its laws, its seasons.

East Coker, the second Quartet, has for its subject meditations on the bondage of nature, on a possible change in our outlook on nature, and the first steps dictated by such a change. The mood is grave as it must be when first we come face to face with our decline. The first reaction to illumination is the unbearable oppression associated with the return into ordinary time, the discontent with our own nothingness. It is the theme of the famous cave dialogue in Plato's *Republic*. The element earth, preponderant in the nature imagery, is felt in the psyche as something dark, heavy and binding; like our own innate inertia. In a way it is the first step which is the most difficult. Later the loss of the old, the loss of the flower in the imperceptible beginnings of a fruition, is envisaged with sombre exultation. Then the character of stifling darkness subtly changes to that of a warm and nourishing womb. But there cannot be arrestment. The process of advance in the dark is travail, and will be the special subject of the third Quartet.

The first movement begins with a reflection on the constancy of matter within the circle of time. The location is the site of East Coker, or any rural settlement. The time is time past, time present and time future in which changes in matter are wrought. Homes go up and crumble, the elements vest different forms, the forms return to dust and rise again. The wheel turns and we turn with it.

'there is a time for building
And a time for living and for generation
And a time for the wind to break the loosened
pane
And to shake the wainscot where the field-
mouse trots
And to shake the tattered arras woven with a
silent motto'.

This stands on its own merit as beautiful poetry, but it
is also a complex symbol. The house is the life that draws
to its close in a circle of time, only to return. Alternatively,
it is the life in which a start is made towards liberation
from this recurrence. And the motto may be the motto of
the Scottish Queen read either way.

'In my end is my beginning.
In my beginning is my end'.

The motto and its reversion are the *leitmotif* of the
second Quartet. In man lies the possibility of further
evolution, but it is by no means granted, and it is not
mechanical. Together the two mottos are as a closed circle,
joined in a grip from which there will be no escape.
'Everything goes, everything returns, eternally turns the
wheel of being', Zarathustra said. But then, again in conjunction, they may mean exactly the opposite, a thought
which Lao Tse expressed like this: 'Failure is the founda-
tion of success, and the means by which it is achieved.
Success is the lurking place of failure; but who can tell
when the turning-point will come'? It is always through a
refusal of his limitations that man comes to the door of
something new. The refusal is often the fruit of suffering,
and most certainly brings with it new suffering of a different kind. Self satisfied lives are not evolving. When man
comes to the end of his former truth, he is on the threshold
of a new truth. Finally, the extinction of his desire for life
within the circle of our time-consciousness is the beginning
of his end here, but at the same time it inaugurates the
beginning of a new state of being.

'In my beginning is my end. Now the light falls
Across the open field, leaving the deep lane
Shuttered with branches, dark in the afternoon,
Where you lean against a bank while a van passes,
And the deep lane insists on the direction
Into the village, in the electric heat
Hypnotised. In a warm haze the sultry light
Is absorbed, not refracted, by grey stone.
The dahlias sleep in the empty silence.
Wait for the early owl'.

A sleeping world, and we somehow feel that this is
goodbye. A few hints suggest the village, and the village
suggests all of England; such beauty beheld with tender-
ness and sorrow! *Partir, c'est mourir un peu*. But in order to
find we must first lose.

Evening falls, and then night. From afar we may espy
the ghosts of dancing villagers upon the common. The
poet admits that the scene has been inspired by the myth
of 'Germelshausen', a German village banned by the Pope
and whose inhabitants came to a ghostly life but one night
a year. The feeling of this passage is one of affectionate
derision, but also blunt, unsparing satire. Here is human-
kind held in the circle of time, striving to bring dignity to
its animal joys and ecstasies.

'The association of man and woman
In daunsinge, signifying matrimonie –
A dignified and commodious sacrament.
Two and two, necessarye coniunction'.

At first we watch, enchanted like those lost in the age-
old dream of Midsummer Night. The dance is of Maya.
The couples, pillars of the edifice of space-time, replicas
of principles that move the atoms. But with:

'Lifting heavy feet in clumsy shoes,
Earth feet, loam feet'.

the mood becomes detached, then strikes home with the
sombre force of a medieval *memento mori*.

28

'The time of the coupling of man and woman
And that of beasts. Feet rising and falling.
Eating and drinking. Dung and death'.

Defining the human situation this forestalls what is to
come: the desire for redemption from it all.

Then four lines introduce a different mood. The night
is past, the journey draws closer. Something fresh and
exciting calls as the sea breeze wafts inland.

'Out at sea the dawn wind
Wrinkles and slides. I am here
Or there, or elsewhere. In my beginning'.

Every instant of time is a closed door towards infinity.

Movement two reminds us that within the circle of time
death is inevitable, and that death is inevitably cata-
strophe, every disintegration a temporary return to chaos.
The apocalyptic vision of a Kalpa, or world-period coming
to an end is preceded by a cryptic description of seasons
being thrown into disorder.

'What is the late November doing
With the disturbance of the spring
And creatures of the summer heat,
And snowdrops writhing under feet
And hollyhocks that aim too high
Red into grey and tumble down
Late roses filled with early snow?'

This seems to me to be a way of saying that aspiration
towards voluntary death in sacrifice is felt to be something
dangerous, even unlawful, contrary to the natural course
of things. Whether we live subject to nature, or whether
we strive to dominate our nature and learn sacrifice, we
know nothing, and we advance in the dark. The second
part of the movement examines old age, the coming face
to face with disintegration. In ordinary life old age brings
neither wisdom, nor peace, only fear of the imminent
falling-asunder, or else hebetude and increased un-

consciousness. Man who advances towards consciousness in voluntary sacrifice advances no less in the dark. To assert the contrary is to delude oneself and others. Voluntary death, man has always felt, may lead to something he cannot now imagine. But whether moving in a circle of recurrence, or whether moving onward the way is fraught with dangers in the dark.

> 'not only in the middle of the way
> But all the way, in a dark wood, in a bramble,
> On the edge of a grimpen, where is no secure foothold,
> And menaced by monsters, fancy lights,
> Risking enchantment'.

Many are the dangers of the way against nature, but the most serious of them all is pride. It is well that here we are reminded:

> 'The only wisdom we can hope to acquire
> Is the wisdom of humility: humility is endless'.

In a scene that recalls the medieval mystery plays a procession of individual types vanish into death and oblivion.

> 'into the silent funeral,
> Nobody's funeral, for there is no one to bury'.

The cross-sections were illusory, the funeral is illusory, vanishing of what never existed.

If a two-dimensional being were told that the moving boundaries of discs appearing, growing, decreasing, and vanishing on its plane are the phenomenal aspect of cross-sections of a being called man; if, in addition, someone were to hint at what man, in his complexity, is, such a plane-being would be much puzzled and at a loss. Perhaps, if it were not angered at being made to feel insignificant, even non-existent, it might even be much excited. If, moreover, it were to deduce that it belongs itself to such a body of higher dimensions that might well change all its views, and deeply affect its manner of living. What has never been cannot perish. But the recognition of the illusory nature of a former state cancels a former world, and is equivalent to the experience of a death. That is the price of the discovery, and it will have to be paid in small coin day by day for all remaining time.

The insight into illumination has led to this point. It is here that, with the poet, we put our feet on an entirely different path. The advance, to which special attention will be given in the next Quartet, the great journey begins at home with a decision, and with preparations. The decision is taken at this moment. It is acceptance, in humility, of the vision, and of the consequence of vision.

'I said to my soul, be still, and let the dark come upon
   you
Which shall be the darkness of God'.

In the famous seventh book of the *Republic* Plato describes the return from a special state into ordinary time. Using the optical simile he likens it to redescent into a dim cave out of sunshine, and to the protracted blindness that this would entail. Mystical literature abounds with such descriptions. One of the best is found in the Tao Te King: 'All men are radiant with happiness, as if enjoying a great feast, as if mounted on a tower in spring, I alone am still, and give as yet no sign of joy. I am like an infant which has not yet smiled, forlorn as one who has nowhere to lay his head. Other men have plenty, while I alone seem to have lost all. I am a man foolish at heart, dull and confused. Other men are full of light; I alone seem to be in darkness. Other men are alert; I alone am listless. I am unsettled like the ocean, drifting as though I had no stopping place. All men have their usefulness; I alone am stupid and clownish. Lonely though I am and unlike other men, yet I revere the Foster-Mother, Tao'.

It is, however, from a great master of the spiritual life within the Christian tradition that Eliot draws at this juncture. This is in keeping with the unity of the *Four Quartets*, and all the poet's penitential poetry. First the poet introduces three examples of his own to describe the new condition. It is followed by beautiful stanzas recalling the style of St. John of The Cross. Then a short recall of the ecstasy, and the movement ends with a variant on the maxims of the *Ascent of Mount Carmel* by St. John of The Cross.

In the new life, a man finds himself, even while living in the world, to be as one sitting in the dark, waiting:

> 'As, in a theatre,
> The lights are extinguished, for the scene to be changed
> With a hollow rumble of wings, with a movement
>   of darkness on darkness,
> And we know that the hills and the trees, the distant
>   panorama
> And the bold imposing façade are all being rolled away–'

So much of a man's former values and convictions, of his opinions concerning himself, and the world perceived as lying outside him is cancelled at the beginning of the new way. So much that to three-dimensional thinking and feeling seemed true and important now loses its meaning, and the fact that these perceptions and desires, having lost their validity, yet continue, and that the momentary vision is, at times so elusive, almost forgotten, unsettles and puzzles such a man most of all. He has lost the old; he has not found the new. He is now between two worlds. At the same time his sensibilities have been, for reasons probably unknown to modern psychology, both sharpened and increased. Consequently he suffers much, and suffers alone. The nature of his suffering is incommunicable; to begin with he understands it very imperfectly himself, and men with world-values would not understand it at all. Only humility and patience can help a man over this impasse.

> 'I said to my soul, be still, and wait without hope
> For hope would be hope for the wrong things;
>   wait without love
> For love would be love of the wrong thing; there
>   is yet faith

But the faith and the love and the hope are all in
the waiting.
Wait without thought, for you are not ready for
thought:
So the darkness shall be the light, and the stillness
the dancing'.

And for the moment we are consoled and uplifted, as we
sometimes momentarily will be during the dark passage of
the negative way, by the aroma of ecstasy in four hints,
four masterly touches. It is through beauty in nature and
such beauty transformed into art that God will speak to us.

'Whisper of running streams, and winter lightning.
The wild thyme unseen and the wild strawberry,
The laughter in the garden, echoed ecstasy
Not lost, but requiring, pointing to the agony
Of death and birth'.

Knowingly, lightly they caress the senses, but the lover
reminds us without delay of the deeper sense and final
lesson of pleasure and delight. There is not, to my knowledge, in the Christian tradition a writer who shows a
better understanding of the meaning of human joy in
natural beauty except St. Francis of Assisi; the poet goes
back to classical and oriental inspiration, but primarily in
qualities grounded in the essence of his own character.

It is not, I believe, accidental that the third movement
ends with a converted passage of the Spanish master. Man,
when he enters upon the negative way, must seek instruction, and must not remain in isolation. Such isolation
would prove a very great strain on the psyche. Others who
have gone by the same path, and who have passed on the
accumulated experience of mankind, can help. The greatest
luck that can befall a man at this point is indeed the discovery of one who can help in this manner. The foregoing
stanza was sweet and tentative. From now on the rhythm
is sure and emphatic like the fall of hammer on anvil in a
galley. We are taken the whole way, and we are spared
nothing.

'To arrive where you are, to get from where you are not,
  You must go by a way wherein there is no ecstasy.
In order to arrive at what you do not know
  You must go by a way which is the way of ignorance.
In order to possess what you do not possess
  You must go by the way of dispossession.
In order to arrive at what you are not
  You must go through the way in which you are not.
And what you do not know is the only thing you know.
And what you own is what you do not own
And where you are is where you are not'.

The subject of the fourth movement, here as in every one of the Quartets, is actual death. He who has seen a loved being waste away in a hospital ward will receive its full impact like no other man. Here, as so often, Eliot uses shock to keep our æsthetic sensibilities at a high pitch. After the distant, the familiar; after the lofty, the commonplace; after the theoretical, a reminder of naked facts. From the remote and medieval this is a brutal recall. The cloying smell, imponderable yet triumphant over antiseptics. The dreadful tidy drabness, the hopeful hopeless self-pity on faces inward with the concentration on a pain. The isolation of suffering. The unseeing chaff and boredom of the staff. The petrified wait by the long agony. It is with us with 'such permanence as time has'. In here all must die, and the only final release from dying is death. The 'wounded surgeon' and the 'dying nurse'; the teachers and the taught, the helpers and the helpless, all.

'the absolute paternal care
That will not leave us, but prevents us everywhere'.

corresponds to the laws that govern the whole complex of dimensions of which the laws that govern our dimension are an immutable part. It is this: in the present state we come up against a wall wherever we turn. Many are the utopias, many the methods of escape, but the truth is that we can never be free. This very fact, at the same time, is

34

our only hope of ever sufficiently desiring to, and thereby succeeding in leaving the rut of time.

At the extremity of dying we are met and uplifted by a strange esoteric simile:

'The chill ascends from feet to knees,
The fever sings in mental wires.
If to be warmed, then I must freeze
And quake in frigid purgatorial fires
Of which the flame is roses, and the smoke is briars'.

It is like peering into a retort, and seeing agony as a chemical compound changing from a troubled seething grey into the rosy-red and reds that hold the sunlight on and under earth. The same thing is repeated in terms of the Eucharist; life blossoms from the life surrendered.

'The dripping blood our only drink,
The bloody flesh our only food:'

For the time-imprisoned multitudes there would be no hope at all if the divine intelligence did not come to our midst, and show the only way. It is true that they, in an almost intentional blindness, see nothing, and understand nothing, clinging to their dimension.

The poem goes on:

'In spite of which we like to think
That we are sound, substantial flesh and blood –'

but then:

'Again, in spite of that, we call this Friday good'.

The perversion is not complete. Evil whose power, it would seem, now reaches further than at any time during recorded history, has not won the battle. The object of Evil, of course, is to sever mankind from its higher possibilities, and to reduce its knowledge to that of the present dimension. Evil, in its lesser aspect is simply ignorance; in its more potent aspect it is the complete inversion of such truth as men of higher consciousness have brought to mankind.

35

The very idea of voluntary sacrifice is the cornerstone of the pseudo-religions, or substitutes for religion by which men of our times are supposed to live. In these surrogates for religion, or philosophy in the sense here understood, the idea is severed from its inner meaning, from connection with a second birth, and is sponsored for purely material reasons. This is done because human society cannot subsist without mutual sacrifice of its members. The emphasis now rests on a better future in time. But since sacrifice is contrary to the natural man, or shall we say to the perverted man, it must now be enforced by many new laws, and, in the extreme form of pseudo-religions, by limitless terror. Mankind unconsciously chastises itself for past omissions. Having sacrificed too little when the choice was free it now invents compulsion. Under pressure both good and evil increase; the tares shoot up with the wheat, and threaten to stifle it altogether; unconscious processes are so much easier and quicker than conscious ones. Meanwhile man learns the bitter lesson that servitude to himself and his blasphemous temporal ideals is slavery, while servitude to God was freedom. Dimly the masses know these things, and distrust themselves and their powers, while the intellectuals are wrangling, and slowly awakening from a fool's dream of an age of reason.

With the fifth movement, as in the fifth movement of *Burnt Norton*, the poet returns to the subject of his art, and sums up his position in this, our present world. With candour he speaks of his difficulties as an artist, a man, and a member of a seemingly doomed historical period. He reflects humbly, for his concern here is with poetry as a receptacle of the voice of the mysteries. Though he feels not worthy, shall he assist without a struggle while the forces of evil completely clog the access to our higher lives? The voice of a poet reaches far, and, if he is a great poet, speaks to different levels of men in their own terms. Our times singularly lack spiritual teachers. We are almost entirely alone, exposed to the 'shrieking voices of temptation'. Shall he, in the face of overwhelming odds, do his best? I think the greater humility lies here.

> 'And what there is to conquer
> By strength and submission, has already been discovered
> Once or twice, or several times, by men whom one
>   cannot hope
> To emulate – but there is no competition –
> There is only the fight to recover what has been lost
> And found and lost again and again: and now,
>   under conditions
> That seem unpropitious. But perhaps neither gain nor loss.
> For us, there is only the trying. The rest is not our business'.

This is perhaps the time and place to recall the age and persistence of the mysteries in human civilisations. The myth of the dying and resurrected God has its roots in the earliest recorded cultures. Disfigured and brought down to a lower level, the rite forgotten or the meaning changed, the kernel of the myth is nevertheless preserved and passed on to each succeeding culture. Perhaps it is correct to surmise that it is inherent in the human mind and indestructible. That is our hope. We might be justified in saying that each new culture grew out of, and thrived on the self-realisation of the few, and that without it no culture could survive. The dying God delving into a dark nether-world; or drowned at sea; or torn limb from limb, but blossoming again, blood-red, with the return of spring; the symbols of vegetation, of the seasons, and of sex. Many myths and many voices, yet always the same Voice. The Nazarene came and enacted the mystery play for our sakes. A handful of men saw it, yet the world became its stage. For two thousand years amidst the absurdity, stupidity and criminality, both their own and those of their surroundings, the men who would, have tried to follow and to understand. A culture within barbarism. It is never otherwise. To follow and to understand, and thus to save and to pass on. End and purpose are hidden from us now. 'The rest is not our business'.

The end of this, as of every one of the *Four Quartets*,

returns to the theme of love. The old man stands for a degree of spiritual maturity. Some emotions have been transmuted, some illusions have fallen away. Man begins to feel the interconnections between disjointed phenomena, he loses his sense of separateness as something is now found, now lost; now in the pattern, now in the detail. It is not much; it is, if nothing else, a starting point. And the key, again, is love. It is a love that has already died many deaths. And now, from the warm ring of protective light we are precipitated into the inevitable sequel.

> 'We must be still and still moving
> Into another intensity
> For a further union, a deeper communion
> Through the dark cold and the empty desolation,
> The wave cry, the wind cry, the vast waters
> Of the petrel and the porpoise. In my end is
>   my beginning'.

THE DRY SALVAGES

NOT HARBOUR OR SHORE are the starting points of the impending journey; it begins far inland, and it is a river that carries us towards the sea.

'The river is within us',

It is the flux of time in the consciousness, existing both fragmented and whole. The journey is along time, with time; from a certain point onward, after the river joins the sea, we are made aware of the ocean of time and times as a whole, including all the different times of all beings. But the ocean has another meaning still, and the journey proceeds along time, amidst infinity, and, if man so wills it, into infinity, the multi-dimensional, the 'probably quite ineffable'.

'The sea is all about us;'

The Dry Salvages, like the other Quartets, speaks of a life within the life we know. In the literal sense its subject is life, any life of any man. But within that life a task awaits to be discovered, and everything points towards it: it is the increasingly conscious quest of the development of consciousness into a new dimension. We are shown repetition, escape, and the way of escape. The poem abounds with hints on conditions and methods leading out of the present state, and they all 'point to one end which is always present'; that is to say, to the importance of awareness in the moment, constant self-control.

The poem begins with childhood, the poet's childhood in a strange land that he deems his home. The river is presumably the Mississippi, running through soil of clay, flanked by commercial cities. To the child it brings the first apprehension of flow, rhythm, periodicity, permanence. The image is abandoned. A widening of the conceptions is symbolised by the entering of the river into the sea. We are skirting a shore, and now the beach stands for time, the land we have already, in a sense, left behind, and the ocean stands for the unknown. What we perceive, we now know to be shells and fragments of unknown wholes with unknown fates stranded on the shoal of time.

> 'The sea is the land's edge also, the granite
> Into which it reaches, the beaches where it tosses
> Its hints of earlier and other creation:
> The starfish, the horseshoe crab, the whale's backbone;
> The pools where it offers to our curiosity
> The more delicate algae and the sea anemone.
> It tosses up our losses, the torn seine,
> The shattered lobsterpot, the broken oar
> And the gear of foreign dead men'.

Strange multiplicity of life-forms emerging from the unknown. And the land, as far as the sea's moisture reaches, is not barren.

> 'The salt is on the briar rose,
> The fog is in the fir trees'.

Sandy earth on granite soil and a hardy vegetation, but the fog wafts inland: we forget in time, but the dew of remembrance comes to our forgetting.

Then a description of the sea, perhaps the most magnificent evocation of the whole poem. Voices and sounds. Out of infinity there reel not one, but many times. Underlying the one unimaginable eternity, the cosmic time, heartbeat of the universe.

'And the ground swell, that is and was from the beginning,
Clangs
The bell'.

The second movement, with a sense of profound oppression, meditates this revolving sphere of time, and times within time. This dead cross-section, even on a cosmic scale, is nothing but a nightmare. The rhythm of the sestina, more eloquently than words could do, implies eternal recurrence. It is a chant of sorrow, monotonous and inescapable. The first two lines of the stanzas are a poem in themselves:

'Where is there an end of it, the soundless wailing,
The silent withering of autumn flowers . . .

There is no end, but addition: the trailing
Consequence of further days and hours . . .

There is the final addition, the failing
Pride or resentment at failing powers . . .

Where is the end of them, the fishermen sailing
Into the wind's tail, where the fog cowers? . . .

We have to think of them as forever bailing,
Setting and hauling, while the North east lowers . . .

There is no end of it, the voiceless wailing,
No end to the withering of withered flowers . . .'

none, except the one possibility:

'Only the hardly, barely prayable
Prayer of the one Annunciation'.

The whole sestina is an elaboration of the theme and rhythm. Each line rhymes with the identical line in every other one of the six stanzas, yet nowhere is meaning sacrificed to form. It produces an extraordinary effect of monotonous recurrence suggesting a giant flashing wheel. The flashing of the wheel, the flowing of the river, the tossing of the waves all symbolise the movement of the consciousness fractured into past, present, and future within, and perceiving the boundaries, as it were, of higher dimensional wholes in time as movement in the external world. In a very ancient anecdote some Buddhist Zen monks were watching reeds by a river being jostled by the wind. They put the question: 'Do the reeds move, or is it the wind that moves?' 'It is your mind that moves' was the superior's answer. *The Dry Salvages* deals with the trial by water, which is the ancient symbol for the movement of consciousness in time. Will consciousness suffer shipwreck

41

in this movement of its own making? Will it repeat the journey in all eternity? Or will it reach terra firma, the still point of the wheel within? Will it abide therein? In the stillness of a conscious now the voice of the Annunciation may be heard. Once it has been heard it can become the aim of our life in time. To feel the voice of God in every heart beat, that is the 'occupation of the Saint'.

Although T. S. Eliot is, I believe, a practising Christian convert, members of any Christian church would probably be mistaken if they interpreted the Annunciation in any exclusive sense. The one Annunciation of a higher life to be born in the psyche may become significant to a man through the life of Jesus Christ, but it is a univeral psychological phenomenon. It seems to me that Eliot's adherence to the European Church is rooted in the qualities that cause his loyalty to the land of his forefathers. Is it not the Appolline urge for measure and form; the recognition of our limitations in space-time that make him embrace the boundaries drawn by heredity, both cultural and geographic, and the codes of a given tradition that go with it? Only through the particular can man attain the universal. This view, reflected in the poet's *Notes on a Definition of Culture*, is the application of his vision. A mixture of religions is bad religion; a mixture of philosophies is a powerless potion. The mind is universal and may roam, but man must find his form, and rules to abide by. Although T. S. Eliot will live as a European classic his culture is universal – and indeed in our day there is no excuse for a less inclusive form of culture since all important writings are available in the original and in translation – and the Oriental metaphysics are as much part of his pattern as are Virgil, Plato, and Dante. We are today aware that the myth of the Saviour is much older than the advent of Jesus, and that the shrines of the Great Mother looked out on the Mediterranean in prehistoric times. In Church dogmatism there is no room for recurrence or reincarnation without which mystical philosophy loses its meaning and power. Eliot has come and has knit our cultural inheritance together: he has left out nothing and has denied nothing. In illumination he has seen the relative sum of our dualistic reasonings, that we may arrive at truth by a way of inclusion as much as, in another sense, by a way of negation. Although not a pure bred Englishman, Eliot has roots in a certain definite past, and he has made that past the basis of his present, and of his future. He has realised his part in a given pattern. Doing that wholly and *à fond* has given him a rare understanding of the entire past of the human mind, and has given to the world a poet of universal value.

The second part of the second movement, and the whole third movement return to the new vision of time which belongs to the first Quartet, interpreting it anew, drawing intellectual and moral conclusions.

'We had the experience but missed the meaning,
And approach to the meaning restores the experience
In a different form, beyond any meaning
We can assign to happiness'.

The examination proceeds from an enlightened intellect. The intuition of the whole man, intellectual, emotional, and sensual, of the true nature of time came as a catharsis, because it momentarily did away with the usual limitations. In the ensuing intellectual examination the poet comes to certain conclusions. If the pattern of all that is exists spatially in a fourth dimension, then not only all joy, but all agony is permanent 'with such permanence as time has'. In this pattern we are bound in births and deaths to our ancestors; a sea of shadowy faces, a quivering whole, and we are bound to all organic life since it emerged from the primeval slime. It is you, and you are it. The pleasure, the horror, and the agony. What can you make of that?

What is the meaning of this pattern? It will be well to remember that in a pattern there is neither sequence, nor evolution.

'Which becomes, in the popular mind, a means of
    disowning the past'.

43

There is only significance, or the lack of it. We know from art that every pattern, unless it comes from the mind of a lunatic – and how many lunatics are able nowadays, in the confusion of ideas, to deem themselves artists – has a meaning. Art is significant form. What, then, may be the meaning of the pattern of our past, present, and future in a fourth dimension? It is important to remember that from the fourth dimension onward we must abandon all idea of form. We are in a world of ideas. The pattern is a pattern of no-form. The angles and curves of this mind-pattern are traced by the emotions, thoughts, and sensations of consciousness in time, enslaved by time and struggling to escape from this limitation.

'Time the destroyer is time the preserver'.

Already the voyager is out at sea when he encounters the land he has left behind once more. In the Quartets *The Dry Salvages* looming up before the traveller signifies the last encounter with a world that the poet has always symbolised by stone, sand, drought, dryness and desolation. It leads, in the following movement, to speculation on the probable role of the three-dimensional life-form in the complex of an ineffable harmony. The passage on the relative permanence of time, which is followed by a discussion of the non-existence of the same time from a new viewpoint, is of great beauty.

> 'And the ragged rock in the restless waters,
> Waves wash over it, fogs conceal it;
> On a halcyon day it is merely a monument,
> In navigable weather it is always a seamark
> To lay a course by: but in the sombre season
> Or the sudden fury, is what it always was'.

On the subject at hand there exists, in the literature of the world, nothing comparable in clearness and simplicity to the dialogue between Krishna and Arjuna in the *Bhagavad Gita*. Movement in time, the inevitability, the permanence of movement, the right attitude towards this

44

non-movement, the existence of this movement from a view-point in a higher dimension are the subjects of this dialogue. The poet's own reflections on the journey here have been inspired by extensive reading of the Mahabharata.

We, the phantasms moving through London streets in the first Quartet, moving into the dark in the second Quartet are now out at sea, about to discover the nature, and the purpose of our journey.

The poet showed us, at the beginning of *Burnt Norton*, a universe that includes, besides the one possibility actually realised in time-space, other, latent possibilities for every moment. We can infer that such a universe is not one of rigid determinism. At every instant man has a free choice between several courses of action. He may in time be led to right action by his willingness for sacrifice. It is true that the three-dimensional body is a cross-section of a four-dimensional body, and follows an ephemeral movement along the closed circle, as it were, which is recurrence in time.

'And the way up is the way down, the way
forward is the way back'.

This is a definition of circular movement. But at the same time we are told that there is no movement at all, and no one to be moved.

'You cannot face it steadily, but this thing is sure,
That time is no healer: the patient is no longer here'.

Man, in his present self-feeling, does not exist, nor has he ever existed. He is the broken fragment tossed up by the deep, the voyager, the seaman departing, arriving or perishing; it does not matter.

'Fare forward, travellers! not escaping from the past
Into different lives, or into any future;
You are not the same people who left that station
Or who will arrive at any terminus,
While the narrowing rails slide together behind you;

45

And on the deck of the drumming liner
Watching the furrow that widens behind you,
You shall not think "the past is finished"
Or, "the future is before us".
At nightfall, in the rigging and the aerial,
Is a voice descanting (though not to the ear,
The murmuring shell of time, and not in any language)
"Fare forward, you who think that you are voyaging;
You are not those who saw the harbour
Receding, or those who will disembark" '.

What does matter is the significance of the pattern. In voluntary and conscious self-negation the pattern is wrought from chaos, and the moments of voluntary agony are as the angles and curves of a beautiful design, the harmonies of a marvellous composition. Diminished and annihilated is what never was. Born, and growing is what was from the beginning. Difficult to conceive, easy to say, almost impossible to put into practice.

After this, as in an extremity, all that man can do is to invoke the higher powers. The voyage perilous, the solitude on the fathomless ocean great. And the prayer shall be for the whole; for those who seek, and who already know how to seek; for those who have lost their way –

'Setting forth, and not returning'

and lastly for those who ended

'in the dark throat which will not reject them
Or wherever cannot reach them the sound of the sea bell's
Perpetual angelus'.

The invocation shall be to the

'Lady, whose shrine stands on the promontory',

on the highest peak, at the furthest extremity of land, for she is the mediator between two worlds. The unfolding of a new life is experienced by man as a coming together of the soul. In a sublimation of sexual forces the white light

46

within, the absolute God, has symbolically appeared as woman. Perhaps the Lady is the oldest divinity of mankind. On the half-forgotten site of a Greek colonial settlement, on a steep cliff amidst the mastix, mountain fern, the broom and thyme I saw the wick alight above the paper flowers even yesterday, the rite forgotten and the meaning changed. Or is it changed? Is it not rather a meaning within a meaning, always that? The women mount the steep ascent to the gaudy shrine to pray for their men at sea, and for the blessing of a son. Though they know it not, is it not the prayer of the one Annunciation?

The reader may remember an early poem by T. S. Eliot, at the time judged unique amongst his other works, *La Figlia Che Piange*. Some critics have thought that it was about a statue of a girl which the poet sought in Italian museums and could not find. The poem has the strange evocative power and the elasticity of symbolism. In the present context the girl becomes synonymous with the imaginary aspects of love forsaken for Great Love, her whom the ancients called Urania. The unique mind of an ascetic, mystic and philosopher was even then wholly bent on the search for perfection. The parting, which the girl does not understand, is a necessity. Whether a major or a minor frustration, it is a fruitful one and the Lady, like Beatrice, is a vision that comes with sweetness to ascetic genius. *La Figlia Che Piange* is a Beatrice not lost, but rejected for her own and the poet's sake. Dante lost his lady through death, but the anonymous girl is divided from the poet through life, this life, which is a kind of death, or stillborn state. She has the still unseeing eyes of a graven image. She is lost in the anonymity of this life, but she, too, is given back to her true stature in transfiguration.

The opening of the fifth movement warns of false approaches to the new life, pitfalls of the mind in quest of the unknown. For some types of men the urge comes with an emotional desire for the mysterious, the miraculous, and such men often turn to all kinds of pseudo-occult or pseudo-scientific pursuits.

47

'Pastimes and drugs, and features of the press:'

from spiritualism to psycho-analysis, nourished by time-born fears and hopes, they are merely a new guise for the old ego-centricism.

'Men's curiousity searches past and future
And clings to that dimension. But to apprehend
The point of intersection of the timeless
With time, is an occupation for the saint –
No occupation either, but something given
And taken, in a lifetime's death in love,
Ardour and selflessness and self-surrender'.

For the first time the poet mentions permanence of the new state. And it is a permanence founded in this life. But immediately he returns to that which is practical, and which concerns us, in our present state. Ecstasy given and withdrawn comes to us through the medium of nature and of art.

'For most of us, there is only the unattended
Moment, the moment in and out of time,
The distraction fit, lost in a shaft of sunlight,
The wild thyme unseen, or the winter lightning
Or the waterfall, or music heard so deeply
That it is not heard at all, but you are the music
While the music lasts'.

This is the gift, and the response required from us is condensed into five words. It is an education leading to constant awareness, covering a whole cycle, and probably several cycles of psychological schooling.

'These are only hints and guesses,
Hints followed by guesses; and the rest
Is prayer, observance, discipline, thought and action.
The hint half guessed, the gift half understood, is
Incarnation'.

If life in time were a mechanical process there would be no hope at all, and no free will for good or evil. Life would have no more meaning than the movement of a row of pistons in a factory. It is the freedom of choice that may lead out of what, to the temporal brain, presents the appearance of a mechanical oscillation. With these reflections the close of the movement draws near and again, as in the foregoing Quartet, it brings an intimation of what is to follow. We are not, as long as we make any effort at all, amongst those 'forever bailing, setting and hauling', nor amongst those swallowed up by the 'dark throat' of the sea. These closing lines touch on the unsolved mystery of reincarnation, and in them there already sounds a note of homecoming. The still green graveyard of an English village suggests what a sweet rest may mean after the toil and dangers out at sea.

> 'And right action is freedom
> From past and future also.
> For most of us, this is the aim
> Never here to be realised;
> Who are only undefeated
> Because we have gone on trying;
> We, content at the last
> If our temporal reversion nourish
> (Not too far from the yew-tree)
> The life of significant soil'.

LITTLE GIDDING

LITTLE GIDDING is the culmination of the poem; it is an
end; and a beginning, and it sums up the whole work
anew. Intellectual difficulties are most evident in the first
and the third Quartets. After that there is a break, and
through the completed act of faith they seem removed in
the fourth. A feeling of a greater rhythm and a different
knowledge is conveyed. Yet *Little Gidding* is the most
esoteric of the *Four Quartets*. It has many common traits
with *Ash Wednesday* and the *Chorus of the Rocks*. To many
people it will come as something familiar because in style
and rhythm it resembles the great religious scriptures of
Christianity. On the face of it, it seems the easiest of the
Four Quartets and this is part of the general plan. It is the
same people who do not see the great esoteric aspects of
the sacred writings, because they assume that they understand; they are content with one meaning where the meaning is serial and inexhaustible. The subject of *Little Gidding*
is love, the love which we were told in *East Coker* to await
without love. Now, purified from the taint of personal
emotion, this love breaks out; the golden unscorching fire
of the Pentecost leaps from every line, and at the end of
the poem condenses into a conflagration in which all
otherness shall be absorbed.

The first movement, again employing elemental symbolism, hints at a new advent; new only in the sense of a
deepening and intensification of what man knows in
simple human happiness, of what came as an airy
messenger, a stony sorrow, and trial by the sea to him who
has put his foot on the path. Imponderable and unspoken
there is an interval between it all and what is to come; the
pentecostal fire. Remember, it came after the bitter death.
We are made to look into a breathless blinding winter
landscape, one instantaneous duration, infinitely remote
from the world of generation. It conveys something given,
but also something ravished from heaven: not grace this

50

time, not the free gift to indicate a way, not sudden and departing, but the fruit of long sustained effort, coming and going it is true, but imparting a new permanence. It is the twelfth hour of the passing year, or the first hour of the new. A traveller has come home and he sees the land of his fathers with new eyes.

'Midwinter spring is its own season
Sempiternal though sodden towards sundown,
Suspended in time, between pole and tropic.
When the short day is brightest, with frost and fire,
The brief sun flames the ice, on pond and ditches,
In windless cold that is the heart's heat,
Reflecting in a watery mirror
A glare that is blindness in the early afternoon.
And glow more intense than blaze of branch, or
    brazier,
Stirs the dumb spirit: no wind, but pentecostal fire
In the dark time of the year. Between melting and
    freezing
The soul's sap quivers. There is no earth smell
Or smell of living thing. This is the spring time
But not in time's covenant. Now the hedgerow
Is blanched for an hour with transitory blossom
Of snow, a bloom more sudden
Than that of summer, neither budding nor fading,
Not in the scheme of generation.
Where is the summer, the unimaginable
Zero summer?'

This is a question still. The last, like the first Quartet, speaks to us of illumination, of a new insight; the stillness termed in Buddhism the self-nature of all beings. It will encroach upon the lives of the disciples, it will make them steadfast in resolve to disregard world-values at all times. Henceforth they carry with them the indelible touch of the mystic fire.

'If you came this way',

If you felt the pull of a new gravity strongly enough, if you came with your life shattered between your hands, if you came as one searching for he knew not quite what, or as one driven by the urge for experience and information; you might start from any point in time and space, arrive at any time, by any of a thousand routes, and arrive not only at this particular place, but at a great many other places, known or unknown. One thing would be the same anywhere, at any time. Here, or at any shrine of mystical communion where man comes into contact with higher intelligence.

'you would have to put off
Sense and notion. You are not here to verify,
Instruct yourself, or inform curiosity
Or carry report.'

The quest for reality is a quest for we know not what, and the move ahead is hidden all the way. The intellect can be the tool. The intellect can be the obstacle. In the present form of our civilisation it still is more of an obstacle than a tool, and to the half-educated masses an almost unsurmountable obstacle.

The poet surveys the past that has led man to this point of his pilgrimage:

'And what you thought you came for
Is only a shell, a husk of meaning
From which the purpose breaks only when it is fulfilled
If at all. Either you had no purpose
Or the purpose is beyond the end you figured
And is altered in fulfilment'.

So it is with every pilgrimage, with every life; totally unconscious and aimless, or else dedicated to a purpose, selfish or disinterested. If man seeks out an ideal that will receive and redeem his self, family, nation, creed, science, mankind, the ideal may, or may not, fail him. The greater probability is that it will. It will be more correct to say that in his ideal man failed himself, because either for himself, or purely ideologically he expected from the temporal a virtue that can pertain to the eternal alone. It is thus that dedication to a world-ideal without insight into its purely symbolic value exposes man to bitter disillusionment, and to the constant danger of inner shipwreck. The moment the scales fall from his eyes he 'plucks that flower safely out of that nettle, danger'. Henceforth, wherever he looks the world of phenomena turns to a world of symbols, meaningless and obtuse at times, translucent and of varied meaning at others, according to his state, but existing *per se* no longer. To see the name of God in everything: the idea survives, fossilised, nearly forgotten in the mystical philosophy of the Cabbala, encyphered in a system of numbers and syllables that perhaps no one can disentangle fully any more, though the principle is simple enough. In the natural life we are together, but solitary we remain. In the mystical life man is alone, but how, and in what manner he is alone his nearest and dearest never know. How, and in what vision he is united to those who, like him, have felt another life in these minor deaths men of natural vision can never guess. And the mystic will admit the leadership of those who have gone before him, and who have gone the whole way. *Little Gidding* speaks of mystical communion, and of the necessity of instruction and common effort. The discovery of symbols is the beginning of man's spiritual growth.

Little Gidding, the site of this particular pilgrimage stands for all shrines of mystical communion, for common effort and within its framework, individual gnosis. Desire for liberation rallied the members of Ferrar's community from all sides around one man, their common centre of gravity. The outward form of their endeavour, like all else in time, came to an end, became:

'A symbol perfected in death'

But the traveller returned, not to the village, to the cottage or mansion of his forebears, but to this place:

'Where prayer has been valid',

53

to the midst of those who knew how to pray, and here united, not alone, receives his Pentecost. Spiritual parentage claims him now, more binding in the world of mind than that of chromosomes.

> 'And what the dead had no speech for, when living,
> They can tell you, being dead: the communication
> Of the dead is tongued with fire beyond the language
>   of the living'.

This refers entirely to mystical life in death. It is, to begin with, acknowledgment of what instruction may be found in life, from people in, but not of the world. In it, too, the poet joins the great and universal tradition of mystical writing, so strange and meaningless from the outside, blazing with living fire once we have the key. In the inner sense this is beatific vision at one with the dead, those who, in sacrifice, have passed from generation.

The second movement admits the death. It had to be. Without it the introductory movement could not have been written. The symbol used is the final dissolution of the elements, and with them, life in time. By vesting form, and with form, consciousness, the elements emerged from chaos and became vehicles of the one evolution. *Morto io, morte il mondo* says an Italian regional proverb. With each death, final or temporary, the universe of time closes its eyes. The key lines of this passage remind us that what we refuse to give freely, will be taken from us without return, and that by clinging to time we 'sacrifice our great possibilities for the little present'.

> 'Water and fire deride
> The sacrifice that we denied'.

> 'The death of hope and despair'

is a line that occurred in *Ash Wednesday*. To us, in our ordinary state, the absence of sadness felt in these three stanzas is something awe-inspiring, something from which we recoil in fear. We now see clearly that we can never divide opposites, we cannot have the one and leave the other. Sorrow and joy as we know them cleave like flesh to bone, and to abandon the one is to abandon the other. And so, in spite of having been made witness of the vision we now face the price that must be paid with a pang of dismay. We experience the helpless shock, the appalling sense of mystery that comes to us when first we stand by a loved one folded into death.

> 'Ash on an old man's sleeve
> Is all the ash the burnt roses leave.
> Dust in the air suspended
> Marks the place where a story ended.
> Dust inbreathed was a house –
> The wall, the wainscot and the mouse.
> The death of hope and despair,
>   This is the death of air'.

We convince ourselves that the 'old man' is the dying god; yet it remains obvious that a poem is the universally valid essence of personal experience; that what has been said again and again had first to be lived, and betrays the most appalling suffering of a kind that is, in its later stages, outside the pale of our pains and agonies. It is the beauty of the verse that reconciles, transmutes our dismay into the inexplicable certainty that, in spite of the horror and the mystery, all is for the best. That at the bottom of the void is all, and much more of the beauty and harmony of art.

The following soliloquy, or dialogue, written in the metre of the *Divine Comedy* takes up the motif of a poet's meeting with one that went before him. We go perhaps not far wrong if we surmise that the poet, on the purgatorial dawn, comes face to face with his own poetical past, embodied as the 'compound ghost' of his own outgrown personalities, and at the same time that of many dead poets beyond whose influence and opinions he has passed. The backdrop is the bombed and smoking streets of a London dawn before the All Clear has sounded. We are at the close of a recurring cycle: the hope that it should be a final end has risen like a pale dawn.

> 'In the uncertain hour before the morning
> Near the end of interminable night
> At the recurrent end of the unending'

a very strange meeting takes place:

> 'I caught the sudden look of some dead master
> Whom I had known, forgotten, half recalled
> Both one and many; in the brown baked features
> The eyes of a familiar compound ghost
> Both intimate and unidentifiable.
> So I assumed a double part, and cried
> And heard another's voice cry: "What! are *you* here?"
> Although we were not. I was still the same,
> Knowing myself yet being someone other – '

The many fleeting selves; the poetical past and the poet's present thus

> 'trod the pavement in a dead patrol',

for art is the warden whose *raison d'être* is to oppose consciousness, the 'moment in and out of time', to the daemonic chthonic powers of nature, ruled by the laws of polarity, who dictate so much more of human behaviour than we admit to ourselves. We are reminded not only of the Dantesque fires, but of the Buddha's Fire Sermon in the *Waste Land:*

> 'Burning, burning, burning, burning'

The flames are the fires of self-love, and art the accidental approach to insight into the illusory nature of separation and desire. It is a way which contains, but does not assure the possibility of inner growth through decrease. Both art and the artist must pass through recurring cycles of discarding the old and giving birth to new forms. Eliot himself has said of the poet:

> 'What happens is a continual surrender of himself as
> he is at the moment to some thing which is more valu-

able. The progress of an artist is a continual self-sacrifice, a continual extinction of personality'.

In the Quartets it is put this way:

'Last season's fruit is eaten
And the fullfed beast shall kick the empty pail.
For last year's words belong to last year's language
And next year's words await another voice'.

Since the *Doppelgänger* has recalled him it is as well to survey the situation. What is the situation of the artist who draws no conclusions from his vision, who rests content with accidental illumination of a greater or lesser degree, who refuses to complete the artistic with the moral effort? What is the situation of him whose art has become the expression of a faith, and of a way of living that affects the whole man? T. S. Eliot thinks he has discovered that the accidental release from time through inspiration is but the possible beginning of a long and arduous path; that most of art in the most recent of human civilisations is but as a tossing in our sleep when the hour of awakening is near. Genius itself, when not accidentally precipitated into a special state, is ordinary man with ordinary foibles, not conscious, for 'to be conscious is not to be in time'. He is moved, made and unmade by the powers of the natural world and as such the prototype of the soul in hell, the melancholy phantom with the 'brown baked features' that the poet met a moment ago. This is a very complex subject altogether. In some works of art the presence of another life is felt as a painful absence.

The meeting in the nether-world was, after all, one between disciple and master. The master holds up a mirror and this is what the lesser sees:

'Let me disclose the gifts reserved for age
To set a crown upon your lifetime's effort.
First, the cold friction of expiring sense
Without enchantment, offering no promise
But bitter tastelessness of shadow fruit
As body and soul begin to fall asunder.

Second, the conscious impotence of rage
    At human folly, and the laceration
    Of laughter at what ceases to amuse.
At last, the rending pain of re-enactment
    Of all that you have done, and been; the shame
    Of motives late revealed, and the awareness
Of things ill done and done to others' harm
    Which once you took for exercise of virtue.
    Then fools' approval stings, and honour stains'.

Why return and stay in the burning city amidst the
values, motives and desires of men who know little outside
the consciousness in time? It is to bear witness of truth as
he perceived it, and the motif is love. But for love not a
word of the *Four Quartets* would have been written. And
the truth begins with truthfulness about oneself, to oneself,
and will be followed by penitence, by faith.

'From wrong to wrong the exasperated spirit
    Proceeds, unless restored by that refining fire
    Where you must move in measure, like a dancer'.

The third movement begins with a meditation on the
present state at the close of a cycle of mortification.
Ordinary thinking moves between the polarity of desire
for life in all its implications, and of indifference towards
life. But at this psychological junction there is a third
possible state:

'Attachment to self and to things and to persons,
        detachment
 From self and from things and from persons: and, growing
    between them, indifference
Which resembles the others as death resembles life'.

Detachment, or non-attachment, as we find it translated
from Buddhist scriptures, is not natural and we know little
about it in the ordinary state. The attached and the in-
different alike are as men immersed. Detachment has
sometimes been likened to a walking on the waters. To be
immersed is to be either possessed, or undone. 'To care,

and not to care' is a great school for the consciousness because it requires intense effort, constant attention and awareness. All our day is a continual 'falling into' situations, people, emotions, ideas, or complete indifference steps into the place vacated by either of these preoccupations. We are rarely outside what happens and we have little control. What is worse, we usually conceive as being outside only as of indifference. Yet if men but knew; the very effort required for the realisation of non-attached care generates force that carries a man far inward into the heart of peace.

> 'This is the use of memory:
> For liberation'.

In the sense here applied it is the constant awareness, unflagging and ever renewed effort to carry self-consciousness from moment to moment. If a man begins to observe not only his behaviour, but the mainspring of his actions he will be surprised to find that for hours, days, years, decades, with occasional interruptions, he is no conscious actor, but a puppet well- or ill-behaved, and that the sum of moments during which he knows himself to exist is very small indeed. In this world of relativity all our measurements proceed from comparisons. Man compares his consciousness to that of lower life-forms, and compared to them he is conscious indeed. Since he cannot make the comparison with what is above him, this is logical and, within limits, justified. Faith is the assumption of a higher ideal, and with it we escape the world of relativity and dualistic logic.

In the remaining pages of The Quartets the poet abandons the theme of love no longer. They are as variations on the closing lines of the *Divine Comedy*. The fruit of memory is

> 'not less of love but expanding
> Of love beyond desire, and so liberation
> From the future as well as the past'.

For the last time we are led onto Arjuna's battlefield,

and the final discourse deals with our attitude to that greater family, mankind, and, in a more immediate sense, our country. Love of a country, no less than personal love, can be but magnified self-love. Lived differently though outwardly the same, it might be the very means of growth through decrease, and a school for right loving. The emphasis is never on the ideal, but on how much of ourselves we bring to it, and in what spirit the offer is made.

> 'Thus love of a country
> Begins as attachment to our own field of action
> And comes to find that action of little importance
> Though never indifferent. History may be servitude,
> History may be freedom. See, now they vanish,
> The faces and places, with the self which, as it
>   could, loved them,
> To become renewed, transfigured, in another pattern.
> Sin is Behovely, but
> All shall be well, and
> All manner of thing shall be well'.

In the light of this saying of one of the greatest English mystics, Dame Julian of Norwich, the limited and half understood ideals of men acquire an equal value with the most enlightened if only the sacrifice is genuine. History is indeed a chain of achievements, of conscious moments intertwined with senseless and unnecessary crimes. Its deeper justification is that it is a battleground where the 'I' learns to overcome itself in service for the sake of a purpose that encompasses, maybe annihilates it, and which is the outer husk of one, hidden at the time. The poet speaks of England, and of those who served her, withholding nothing. This links with the beginning of the fifth movement of *Burnt Norton*.

> 'Only by the form, the pattern,
> Can words or music reach
> The stillness, as a Chinese jar still
> Moves perpetually in its stillness'.

In the pattern of her history England can be likened to the Chinese jar; the conscious moments in the lives of those who served her in any walk of life are as the words, or notes of music.

Connect this with the close of the third movement of *The Dry Salvages* and the message becomes clear as day.

> ' "on whatever sphere of being
> The mind of man may be intent
> At the time of death" – that is the one action
> (And the time of death is every moment)
> Which shall fructify in the lives of others:
> And do not think of the fruit of action.
> Fare forward'.

Conscious moments are those moments when self is obliterated in a greater purpose. But be not attached to the purpose either, that is the key.

The meditation on the role of history ends:

> 'And all shall be well and
> All manner of thing shall be well
> By the purification of the motive
> In the ground of our beseeching'.

We grasp this message better now than when it was first delivered at the close of *The Waste Land*. There it came to us in the forgotten tongue of a remote culture, no more than a hint liable to misinterpretation; it seemed almost an irony after the awful apocalyptic vision.

The fourth movement, with accelerated rhythm, announces the fearful, the desired conflagration. A love for which we are too small demands our surrender. Those who refuse themselves burn in no hell, but in the fire of their self-willed aridity.

> 'The only hope, or else despair
> Lives in the choice of pyre or pyre –
> To be redeemed from fire by fire'.

The logical mind can never cease from questioning the

necessity of suffering. It is perhaps the greatest meta-physical mystery of all. But no answer can be given by logic itself. The answer can perhaps be felt in a new state, but the knowing comes with the doing, not before, and then remains incommunicable.

'Who then devised the torment? Love'.

What can a man make of that in his ordinary self-willed state? But let him silence the self, the silence will be invaded by love, and for a fraction of a second he might know. A drop of that potion will strengthen him for long years.

In the fifth movement, in order to throw into relief the idea of culture as a pattern reaching into stillness, we are reminded that a different state of affairs is not excluded.

'A people without history
Is not redeemed from time, for history is a pattern
Of timeless moments'.

In the present as always there exist on earth communities who had once a culture of their own, but have sunk to a very low level. Some of the existing tribes perhaps have no past at all. At the other extreme there are peoples technically advancing, but deeply immersed in time and time-values. Their history contains a very small element of culture, and is largely made up of the senseless patterns of illusion and crime. This is so because the emphasis of their beliefs is on the getting instead of the giving. It must be extremely difficult for a man to develop within such a society. In barbarous societies, if present at all, the idea of sacrifice degenerates into the killing of innocent people for the sake of a false idol. While the inner evolution of man is hard to register, every society betrays its presence or absence in its individual members by the presence or absence, and the quality of, certain human activities. It is evident that sterile societies however 'vital' they may deem themselves to be on a physical plane, produce nothing vital in philosophy and art, and that their religion, if any, has been superseded by pseudo-religion or religions. 'Timeless moments' are almost absent, and certainly most difficult to experience within the frame of these pseudo-cultures. A moment like the one at the close of movement five, the meditation in the chapel, will be extremely unlikely in a barbarous country, be it savage or modern. There will be no connection with a live past, no knowledge, no inner readiness for the experience, no leisure coupled with awareness, no inner and possibly no outer freedom. Art will be absent or fossilised. Every form of barbarism has its mutations, but these traits are common to all.

In timeless reflection afternoon has moved on, un-noticed, into the smoke-laden hour of a winter dusk.

> 'So, while the light fails
> On a winter's afternoon, in a secluded chapel
> History is now and England'.

Close of a cycle of seasons, of a cycle of history, of a cycle of one life, and spiritual growth within that life; an end and a beginning. A sense of intimacy grows on us. Near the shrine the force that draws the home-coming like a magnetic centre assures us that we, too, are not alone.

> 'With the drawing of this Love and the voice of
>   this Calling
> We shall not cease from exploration
> And the end of all our exploring
> Will be to arrive where we started
> And know the place for the first time'.

Through the Love of God we come to understand how the primitive mind departs from faith on its own level only to return to faith on the apex of its development. This is indeed homecoming. Home is our own most inti-mate being. We are back in the rose garden. What we knew in innocence is what we know in experience. End and beginning meet. All roses are one rose. In emanation are the many, in the return there is only One. Gone the anguish of self-immolation; what seemed a terrifying conflagration is realised as:

> 'A condition of complete simplicity
> (Costing not less than everything)'

The 'everything' we clung to was nothing, the fires burning in a void. The contrast from burning to the unspeakable freshness of this new world comes to us through the use of one of the earliest and most enchanting symbols of medieval thought, the mystic rose.

> 'And all shall be well and
> All manner of thing shall be well
> When the tongues of flame are in-folded
> Into the crowned knot of fire
> And the fire and the rose are one'.